Card Tricks

John Cornelius

SE
Select Editions

First published in Canada in 2002 by
Select Editions
8036 Enterprise Street
Burnaby, BC V5A 1V7
Tel: (604) 415-2444
Fax: (604) 415 3444

ISBN: 1-894905-00-8

Printed in China

10 9 8 7 6 5 4 3 2 1

Contents

Introduction

Nothing is more fun than to entertain others (unless it's being entertained in turn). Not long ago, guests were expected literally to sing for their supper—to sing a song, play a musical instrument or recite a poem to entertain the assembled company after dinner. Today, such opportunities for public performance are fewer, especially for those without obvious musical talent. Yet with a deck of cards, a few simple props, and a little practice, anyone can intrigue and amuse a group with card magic—whether for an impromptu few minutes or a longer, structured piece.

Card magic, along with tricks with dice or cups and balls, probably has its roots in the disreputable but universal practice of relieving simple citizens of their spare cash via any number of skilled moves in which the quickness of the hand did indeed deceive the eye. The human brain is easily lulled into a state of inattention until something unexpected takes place. In this book, all the tricks are strictly for entertainment only: they range from the simple and quick to those requiring practice and some work to bring off.

Even if you are an absolute beginner, this book will provide you with enough material to start your career in card magic almost immediately. By skillfully combining different types of tricks, short and long, you will be surprised how easy it is to fool friends and family, and discover that even if people have an idea of 'how it's done', they actually love to be fooled—a little—if it's done with grace, confidence and good humour.

Most of the tricks in this book require only one deck of cards or more, but with a minimum of expenditure you can add an extra sheen to your act. The essence of successful card magic, however simple the trick, is to appear confident and in control. Being well groomed with clean hands and nails, and dressed and equipped for the job sends a message to your audience that you know what you are doing!

Equipment

- 2 fresh decks of standard playing cards (same back pattern)
- 2 worn decks of playing cards (same back pattern as the fresh decks) for tricks involving damaging cards by bending, marking, tearing, etc.
- 1 forcing deck of duplicate cards (can be all one pip number of one suit, for example, or one pip number per suit of all four suits)
- Piece of green baize cloth at least $1m^2$, to provide a 'stage' on which the card tricks are performed
- Fresh white linen handkerchief or napkin at least $30cm^2$
- Nail scissors or clippers (for clipping cards, but also for keeping nails trimmed)
- Double-sided Scotch tape (for sticking cards together)
- Pen and paper (for 'prediction' tricks)
- Large white envelopes

Clothing

Professional card magicians, whether male or female, often perform in evening dress, either full white tie and tails, or a tuxedo and waistcoat. The reasons are first to look confident and in control, second to maximize the number of pockets in which cards can be hidden! The following items—which should not be close-fitting—can be easily acquired from members of family or from charity shops:

- Dark tuxedo jacket
- Dark waistcoat
- Dress trousers
- White dress or fancy shirt, with smart cuffs

Technical Terms

CUT:
Lift a number of cards, usually a third to a half, from the top of a deck, and place them under the former bottom card.

DOUBLE-BACKED CARD:
Card with two backs and no face. This and the following one are special trick cards not found in a normal deck.

DOUBLE-FACED CARD:
Card with two faces, usually showing different values, e.g. ace of Spades and king of Diamonds.

FORCING DECK:
Deck in which all the cards are the same (e.g. all ace of Spades); or which consists of groups of identical cards.

INDEX CORNER:
One of the corners of a card-face showing its suit and pip value.

KEY CARD:
A specially prepared card that enables you to locate the position of a selected card in the deck.

MAKING THE PASS:
Reversing the position of the upper and lower halves of the deck.

MARKER CARD:
A card used to indicate the position of another card or cards.

ONE-WAY BACK CARDS:
Cards whose back pattern is not a mirror-image of the two halves: you can identify a reversed card. Also known as a one-way deck.

DECK:
The full set of 52 cards.

PACKET:
A set of cards, part of a full deck, taken from the deck.

PIP VALUE:
The number of spots (i.e. suits) on the card. The index pips on the corners are not included in this value.

RIFFLE:
Drawing the finger or thumb smartly across the edge of the deck, making a distinctive sound.

SET-UP DECK:
A deck which you have secretly set up in the sequence you need.

SHORT CARD:
A key card prepared by cutting about 2mm off the end of the card.

STANDARD DECK:
One that has not been tampered with.

STRIPPER DECK:
A deck in which all the cards taper very slightly in width towards one end. They stand out when reversed top to bottom. Useful for identifying cards behind your back. One stripper card can make a useful marker card in an otherwise standard deck.

Basics of Technique

- Get very accustomed to handling the cards. Practise as often as you can, until you can carry out most movements without looking at what you are doing. Keep eye-contact with your audience—don't watch your own movements.
- Keep talking to your audience—talk is a good distraction. Perfect your own line of professional patter and 'business'. Use diversions. While carrying out a tricky movement, ask a question of a spectator. Everyone will look at him, not at you.
- Always make arm and hand movements appear natural and easy. Never lose control of the situation—but pretend to, if you like. Spectators love to be tricked by apparent failure becoming success.
- You need only a few basic props. The professional card trickster will have a waistcoat with pockets, a jacket or tail coat with inside and outside pockets, and trousers with side and hip pockets. A small table is essential. Other useful accessories include: short soft pencil, sheets of paper, napkin, chair.
- Left and Right: Normally in card tricks, a left-handed person can simply read Left for Right in the instructions, and everything works in the other direction.
- To remember cards, go first by value, then by suit, like 10D for ten of Diamonds. If you need to memorize four cards, say 2S, 5D, JS, 10H, memorize the values first—2, 5, J, 10; then the suits, SD, SH.
- Get to know probable behaviour patterns. When a man is asked to pick a suit, he will probably go for Spades; a woman will probably opt for Clubs.
- When a spectator is asked to pick from a range of cards, he or she will almost always go for one side or other of the middle and very rarely to the very middle or the outer edges.
- Use only good-quality cards.

Guide to Sleight of Hand Techniques

1 THE OVERHAND SHUFFLE

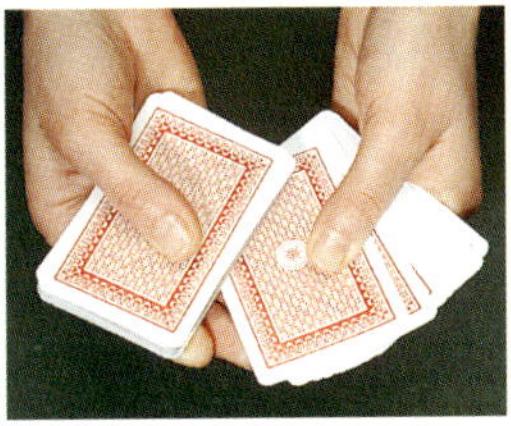

This is the standard shuffle in card-play. Hold the deck in your right hand and pass the cards singly or in small packets to your left, using your left thumb to draw them, and rearranging the order in a random way. However, your rearrangement need not be completely random. The Overhand Shuffle is also a good way of keeping a few cards exactly where you want them to be. Here are some examples:

Keep the top card on top:

Hold the deck in your left hand, face down and angled toward the right. Lift the deck with the right hand, retaining the top card in the left by a slight pressure of the left thumb. Shuffle the other cards on top of this one. Then take the whole deck in your right hand, and shuffle all the cards into your left hand, dropping the last one on top.

Move the top card to the bottom:

Do as above, except that you don't make the final move that would place it back at the top.

Running:

This is ensuring you place a specific number of cards on top of a key or marker card, either at the top of the deck or between marker cards. You draw them one by one in the course of shuffling, using the left thumb, and counting. Practice soon makes this easy.

2 THE RIFFLE

Holding the sides of the deck tightly in your left hand, clip the narrow ends between the thumb and fingers of the right hand. Bring the fingers up

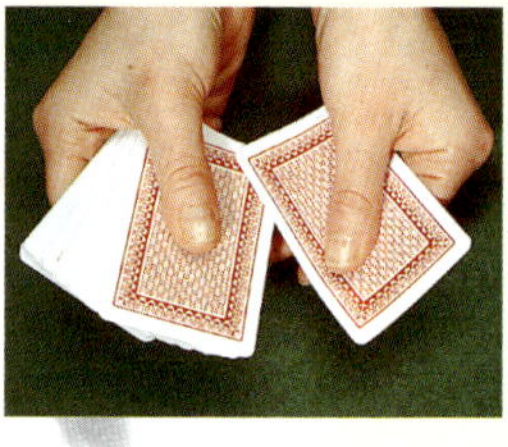

against the face of the deck, so that each card is subject to brief upward pressure and bends slightly, making the typical 'riffle' sound. This is not just a flourish. It can be useful for straightening a previously palmed card. It can also be a diversion —many spectators will believe that the trick takes place somehow during the innocent riffle.

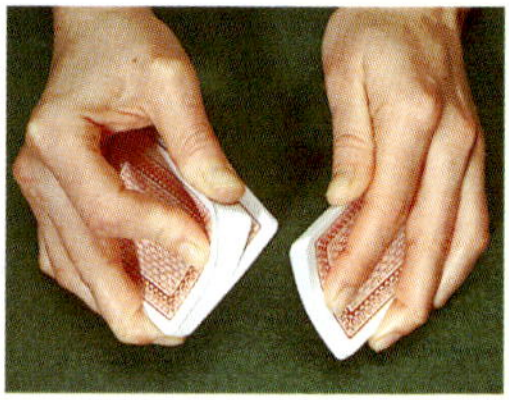

3 THE RIFFLE SHUFFLE

Split the deck into two packets and, with one packet in each hand, merge them into a single deck by allowing each packet to intersect the other. This is also called dovetailing the cards. Use the riffle shuffle to keep chosen cards both on the top and the bottom of the deck. To keep one or more cards on the top, just release them last of all from the right-hand packet. To keep the bottom cards at the bottom, just release them from the left hand in the first movement.

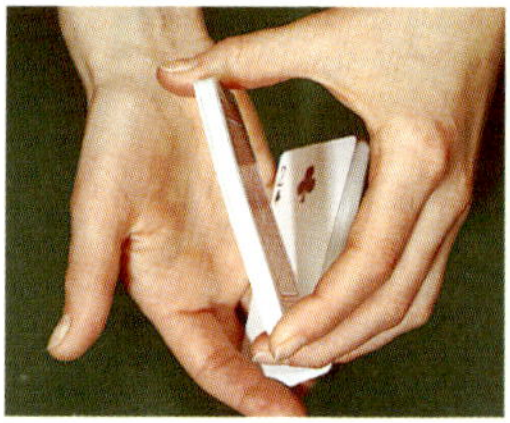

Keeping the deck in your desired order:

Having prearranged the deck of cards to your requirements, cut the deck into two packets, the upper one in your right hand and the lower in your left. In each case your thumb is above the cards and your fingers are below. Place your two packets edge to edge and work the edges of the right-hand cards in between the left-hand ones, fanning the packet slightly in the process. But keep the cards from the right-hand packet protruding about 2.5cm above the left-hand ones. Clip the long edge of the right-hand packet between your thumb and second finger and bend the cards quickly and sharply downwards and outwards. They are released from the left-hand packet and you smoothly slide the right-hand packet on top of the left-hand one, keeping the original order while having apparently done a full shuffle.

4 THE FALSE CUT

Hold the deck over the table, between thumb and second finger of each hand, near one end. Pulling out around a third of the cards from the bottom, transfer them to the top still gripping them between thumb and second finger. With your right third finger, lift about half of the lower packet. Now the cards are separated into three packets. Take your hands apart, letting the top packet drop on to the table, still in original order. On it first drop the packet from your left hand, then from the right. The cards are in their original order but the viewers will have seen you cut them.

5 THE JOG

This is pulling one card a little way out of the deck, so that its position is clear —and so, therefore, is that of the cards on either side. In other words it may be a marker card rather than a key card. Say you want four kings in a row. Start with these on top of the deck. Hold the deck in your left hand and lift the lower half with your right. While preparing to take the cards off with your left thumb, move your right hand about 2.5cm towards your body and draw off a single card. Then move your right hand forward again and carry on with the shuffle. At the end of the movement, one card will protrude from the deck at the inner end, towards you, marking the location of the four kings. To bring these to the top, take all the cards beneath the jogged card, and drop them on to the top, as if you were making a simple cut.

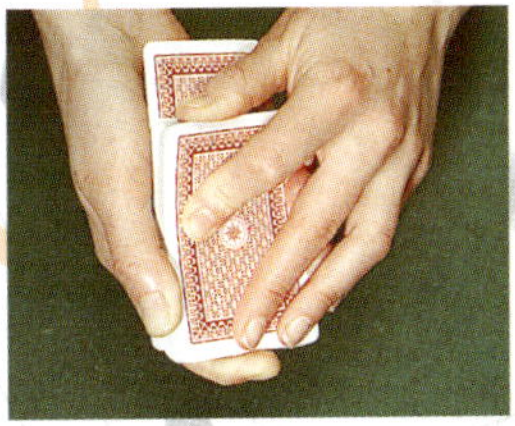

6 PALMING

Isn't it curious that a playing card is just the right size to be concealed in a palm? To keep a palmed card secure, place its opposite corners between the top joint of your little finger and the ball of your thumb. To palm a card from the deck, take the deck in your left hand in the normal position for dealing. Place your right hand over the deck, thumb at the inner end, joints of the four fingers over the outer end. As if squaring the deck, run the fingers and thumb

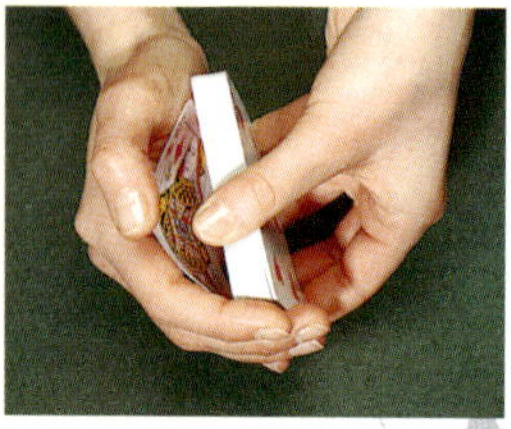

of your left hand over the edges of the cards. Then return your right hand to its original position, and with your left thumb, push the lower end of the top card to the right. With a tiny tensing of your right hand, you can now palm the card. Move the fingers and thumb of your right hand to the right-hand corners of the deck, and straighten the deck with your left hand, then take your left hand away. The palmed card is now in your right hand.

To return the card to the deck, hold out your left hand and have a spectator place the deck on your left palm and cut it. With your right hand, pick up the lower portion of the deck from your left, relax your hold on the palmed card and let it settle on top, then place one packet on top of the other.

7 THE BASIC PASS

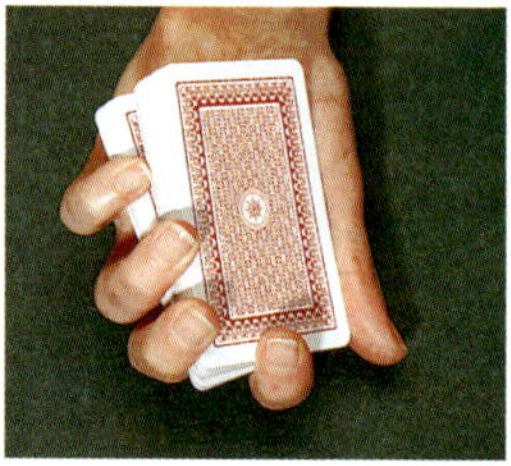

This basic movement is to reverse the position of the top and bottom halves of the pack in your hand, unobserved by the spectators. Hold the deck in your left hand, face down; fingers to the right and thumb to the left. Slide the tip of your little finger in where you want to make the cut, and close the other three fingers on the upper half. Now you will exchange the positions of each packet.

Bring forward your right hand to cover the deck. Grasp the lower packet of cards lengthwise between the second finger and thumb of your right hand. Press the inner edge of the lower packet into the fork of the left thumb. Your left thumb is placed across the upper packet, slightly bent. Now draw away the upper packet a little, held by the fingers of your right hand, by slightly

opening the fingers of your left hand, including the little finger. At the same time lift up the outer edge of the lower packet until the two packets just clear each other. The lower packet rests on the palm of the left hand, the upper packet on the extended fingers. Now by closing your left hand they will be brought together again, but the lower packet will slide on top of the upper and the positions of the two portions will have been reversed.

8 CONTROLLING A CHOSEN CARD

Have a card selected from the deck. To replace it again, cut the deck, holding it face down. Place the chosen card on top of the lower packet and replace the upper packet on top, but with the tip of your left little finger between the two packets. Keep the outer ends of the deck firmly together and riffle the ends a few times.

Take the upper packet in your right hand, thumb at the rear, fingers at the front. Slightly raise this packet, and as you do, drop your left thumb under the lower packet and turn it face up (the chosen card is now at the bottom). Turn the cards in the right hand face up and shuffle on top of the lower. Turn the deck over and continue to shuffle, ensuring that you now keep the chosen card as the top one.

9 NOTING THE BOTTOM CARD

Ask a spectator to shuffle the cards. As he returns the deck to you, take it in your right hand, at the same time, very casually, pull up or adjust your left sleeve or cuff. Then do the same to your right cuff. This is just for balance, to make the action seem normal. However, as you pull your left sleeve or cuff, you have an excellent opportunity to note and memorize the bottom card.

10 FORCING

This is making sure a particular card from the deck is selected by a spectator without him realizing that it has been 'forced' on him. There are different ways of achieving this. Perhaps the most common is to note the bottom card as explained in 9 above, then cut the deck so that the bottom card is about a third of the way up. Hold the deck so that there is a slight break at this place, then run the cards from the upper two-thirds of the deck into a fan, using your left thumb. Invite a spectator to take any card. When you have fanned out about half the deck, slide one card slightly forward, but then take it back, saying, 'It doesn't have to be that one.' Continue to fan until you reach the break, and then slide the force card a tiny bit forward, casually but invitingly, while saying, 'Take any card you please.' The spectator will take the forced card. Needless to say, this manoeuvre needs practice to get its timing right. You must present the card just as his fingers are about to close.

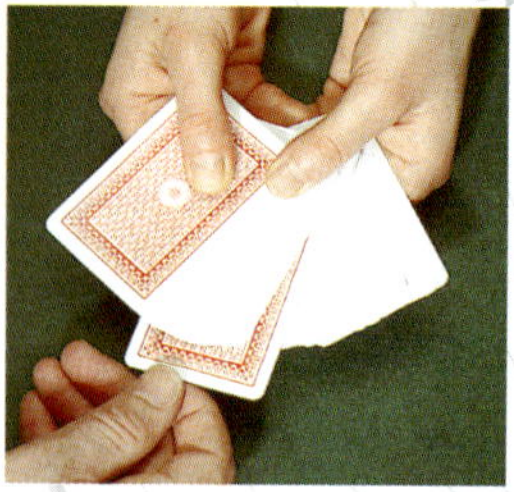

Another way of forcing is to pre-insert a short card near the middle of the deck. The card you want to force is placed just above it in the deck. Once again you ask a spectator to choose any card. Hold the deck straight up in front of him and riffle the deck smoothly from face to back, so that the faces appear in front of him in rapid succession. The card following the short card will register for a split second longer than the others.

11 DOUBLE LIFT

This is lifting two cards at once without being observed. Hold the deck in your left hand, edges squared up, face down. Bring the right hand over, thumb at the rear, fingers at the front. While apparently squaring up the ends, you actually press your fingers against the front of the deck to make it slightly wedge-shaped. Now, using the ball of your thumb, raise the rear ends of the two topmost cards. Slide the end of your left little finger underneath.

With the right thumb-tip at the back of the two cards, and the tip of your right forefinger at the front, turn the cards together and lay them face up on top of the deck, the ends sticking out about an inch from the inner edge of the deck. Show the 'top' card in this position to your spectators, name it, then take the cards at the lower outer corner as before and turn them face down on the back of the deck.

12 GOOD LOCATION

To keep control of a freely chosen card. Hold the fanned-out deck in your left hand and ask a spectator to select any card. As the spectator returns the card to you, pinch the deck so that the returned card cannot be fully inserted. With your right hand, close the fan. The selected card will still protrude slightly. With your right hand, take all the cards beneath the chosen one and shuffle them on top of the deck. The chosen card is now on the bottom of the deck. You can leave it there or bring it to the top, depending on what your trick is to be.

13 MARKING

Making a mark or alteration on a card or cards for purposes of recognition. This can be a tiny mark with a soft pencil, a nick with the thumbnail, or an oblique nail score along the side of the deck showing the run of cards. Such marks are intended to be undetectable by the spectators.

14 THROWING A CARD

Apart from its use in certain tricks, this is a useful way of showing the audience that your cards are normal ones, and impressing them at the same time. Hold the card lightly between first and second fingers of the right hand, with the hand curved inwards towards the wrist. Straighten the hand with a sudden movement, at the same time jerking your arm forward. The card goes spinning off, and the gyration gives it both a long and an even flight.

15 SHOWING AN EMPTY POCKET

If a card is placed in the top inner corner of a trouser pocket, you can carefully draw out the pocket-lining to show that there is apparently nothing in your pocket. Note that jeans or tight trousers are not suitable for tricks which require pocketing.

16 SWITCHING DECKS

This is necessary when you want to exchange a normal deck, which has been seen and checked by the spectators, for a prearranged or set-up deck. Here are three of numerous possible methods. Remember to keep talking as you make the moves:

Place your set-up deck in your left-hand waistcoat pocket:

Holding the standard deck in your left hand, turn toward the table and drop it into your outside-left-hand jacket pocket, at the same time using your right hand to transfer the set-up deck from waistcoat to your left hand. Keep your elbows in while doing this, to minimize movement.

On a chair seat have several sheets of paper, with your set-up deck beneath:

With the standard deck in your right hand, lift the sheets or pick up the top one, at the same time dropping the deck and picking up the duplicate.

Have the set-up deck in your right hip pocket or tucked in your belt:

Find a reason to put the standard deck behind your back in your left hand. With the right hand, extract the set-up deck from the hip pocket, switch decks from hand to hand and slip the standard deck from the left hand into the right hip pocket. A slight turn to the right will help conceal the action.

The Tricks

Prediction

You write the name of two cards on a slip of paper which magically appears between them in a cut and shuffled deck.

Allow a spectator freely to inspect and shuffle the deck. Take it back face up and note the facing card. Hold the deck in the left hand in the normal dealing position. Bring the right hand over the deck to grasp it by the thumb at the end nearest your body and the first three fingers at the other end. The fingers of the left hand now pull the top (memorized) card to the right, around the right edge of the deck, to the bottom (the right little finger has to move to allow this to happen). The card is now reversed beneath the deck. This takes practice to do undetectably.

Place the deck on the table, face up (the reversed card at the bottom will be face down). Memorize the top card. Ask a spectator to cut the deck about two-thirds of the way down, and place the cards face down on the right of the rest of the deck.

Meanwhile, you write your Prediction (the two cards you have memorized), and hand it to another spectator. Now ask the spectator to cut the remaining third of the deck, at about the middle, and place the packet face up to the right of the others. You now have three packets; middle one face down, outer ones face-up. Place the first pile (with reversed card at bottom) on top of the middle pile, and then place both on top of the third pile.

Ask the spectator to remove the face down packet, put it on the table, and cut it into two parts. Ask the spectator with the Prediction slip to place the slip on what was the top portion, and to place the lower portion crosswise on top. The slip is thus between the two cards whose names you wrote on it.

Hold Down that Card

A card, previously chosen by a spectator, mysteriously 'leaves' the deck to appear elsewhere in the room.

Have a standard deck placed face down on the table, after it has been inspected and shuffled. Select a victim and ask him to look at the top card, memorize it, and replace it without telling which one it is. Now ask him to press down hard on the deck with the back of his left hand. To add extra force, he should press down his right palm on his left. Show him how this is done so that he will know. Ask him if he is pressing hard. Then announce that you will make the topmost card leave the deck and appear elsewhere in the room. Remind him to press down as hard as he can, to keep the card from flying away. Then produce the card from an unexpected location.

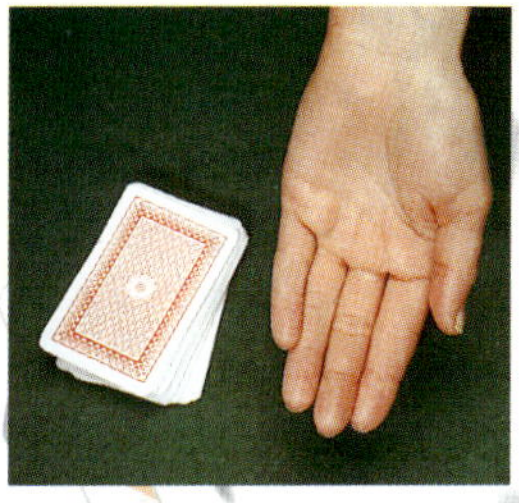

▲▼ *Concealing a card on the back of a hand (above) as it appears to spectators. Below: how it's done.*

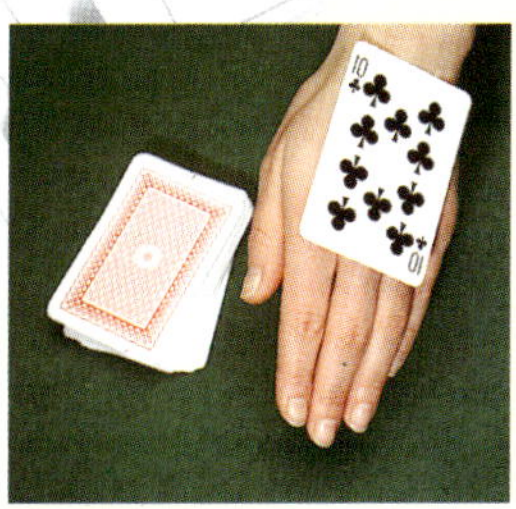

HOW:

The key moment is when you are showing your victim how he should place his hands. You must ensure that the back of your left hand is moistened and pressed down flat, so that the top card, which has already been seen and replaced by the spectator, sticks to it. Then move both hands behind your back, and remove the card with your right hand. While the spectators watch your victim pressing down, drop the card in a pocket, or in a place where you can invite another spectator to discover it.

Whispering Queen

The queen of Clubs 'identifies' four cards. A simple trick to be performed quickly as a warm-up to something more complicated.

Allow a spectator to freely inspect and shuffle the deck. Take the deck and run through it quickly to find and extract the queen of Clubs. While doing so memorize the four top cards which will be at the top of the closed deck (see hint on memorizing cards in Basics of Technique on page 8).

▲ *Slide the queen under each pile in turn—then pretend the queen is 'telling' you each of the bottom cards.*

Ask a spectator to deal out the cards, one by one, into four packets. Watch him lay the first four cards down to ensure you know which is which. Now announce that the queen of Clubs will tell you the bottom card of each set. Slide her underneath each packet, then hold her to your ear, as if she is giving you the information, before you announce the name of each card.

EXPERT TIP ♥ ♣ ♦ ♠ ♥ ♣ ♦ ♠ ♥ ♣ ♦ ♠ ♥ ♣

Keep your fingernails neat and clean if doing card tricks. Unsightly nails will detract from the impact of your magic.

Self-control

Through psychic powers, you select the correct card before the spectator has even thought of it!

Ask a spectator to inspect and shuffle the deck, and to spread the cards face down on the table. He points to any card he chooses, and it is then taken out and kept in view, still face down, in your breast-pocket.

Now ask him to think of and name another card. You reassemble the deck—less the 'decoy' card in your pocket—and run through the cards looking for the one he has named. When you find it, move it to the top position, but say you can't find it.

Ask the spectator to find it, but palm the top card as you pass him the deck. Of course he cannot find the card he named. Place your hand at your breast pocket, push down the first 'decoy' card, then produce the palmed card as if from your pocket.

▲ *Palm the top card as you offer the spectator the deck.*

◄ *Push the 'decoy' card into your top pocket as you 'produce' the correct, palmed card.*

Find the Queen

You correctly identify a card inside a sealed envelope.

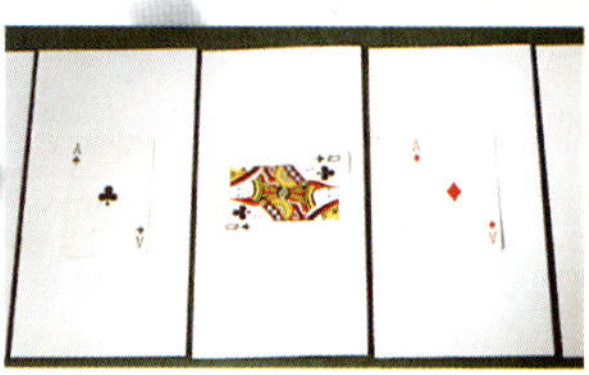

Simple, but mystifying to the onlookers. Tell your audience that you will seal up four aces and a queen in five separate, identical envelopes, and that by telepathy you will be able to pick out the envelope with the queen. Let them watch you place the cards in the envelopes and seal them. But lay the aces on their sides. As you insert the queen, ensure that you turn her to be upright inside the envelope. Now let the spectators shuffle the envelopes. As each one is passed to you, hold it to your forehead, looking immensely wise, hiding the fact that you are feeling to find the positioning of the card inside. When you are given the queen, ensure that you turn her on her side as you open the envelope.

◀ *Insert the aces horizontally.*

▼ *Insert the queen vertically, bending the envelope to hide the action.*

Cards in the Dark

Your telepathic talents will astound your audience—but the trick couldn't be simpler!

Let the spectators inspect the deck and shuffle it thoroughly. Hand the deck to one of them. Now ask for the lights to be put out. When the room is completely dark, ask this person to pass you one card. Name it immediately. When the lights are turned on again, you are found to be holding the card you named.

HOW:

This is managed by palming off a card as you give the deck to the spectator. Note mentally what card it is. Put this card in a pocket. When you are passed a card in the dark, put it in another pocket and take out the one you already know.

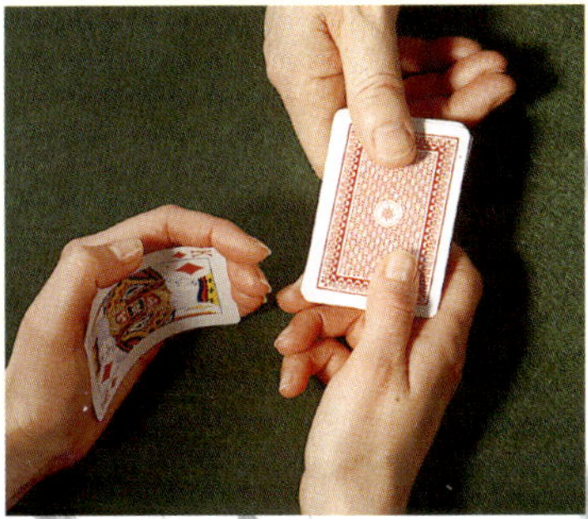

▲ *Palm the top card as you pass the deck to the spectator.*

FURTHER ACTION:

If you can surreptitiously take two or three cards from the deck, and memorize all three in correct sequence, you can immediately repeat the trick with other spectators, to their increasing amazement, while chatting with them about the usefulness of your diet of carrot-juice.

EXPERT TIP ♥ ♣ ♦ ♠ ♥ ♣ ♦ ♠ ♥ ♣ ♦ ♠ ♥ ♣

Cards with a linen finish are easier to handle than cards with a plastic finish.

Magic Dice

Under your control, the tumbling dice reveal an unknown card's exact location.

Shuffle your deck vigorously, offer it to a spectator, and invite him to select any card he pleases, without telling you, and to replace it anywhere in the deck. You then reshuffle the deck and ask him to cut it.

Deal out six rows of six cards each, one at a time to each row. Hand the spectator a pair of dice and a shaker. Let him try out the dice to see that they roll freely. Then ask him to roll each one singly: the first one to give the number of the row, and the second to give the card's position in that row. Suppose he throws a five and a three. The card he noted will be the third card in the fifth row.

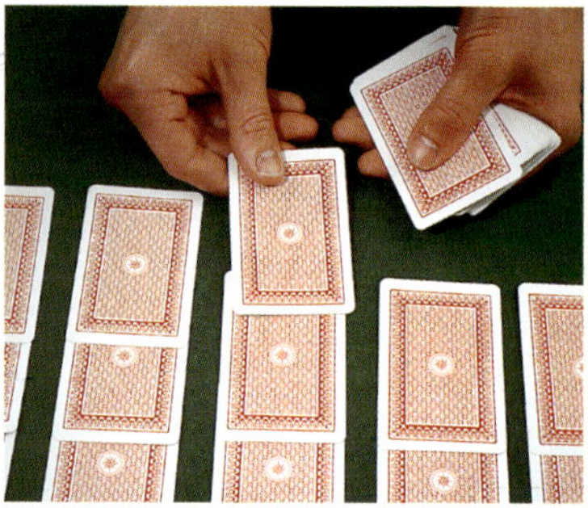

▲ *Deal out six rows of six cards each.*

▼ *Forcing deck of at least 36 identical cards.*

HOW:

This trick requires a forcing deck of at least 36 cards, all the same. Whatever the numbers on the dice, the spectator can only pick up the card he chose. A useful tip is to get the spectator to name his card before picking it up. This enables you to gather up all the other cards, saying

▶ *The dice 'choose' the spectator's card.*

'I think you will find your card is here.' Everyone will look as your victim picks up his card. Meanwhile you are exchanging the forced deck for a standard deck (from which you have removed the card corresponding to the forced deck), and you can casually place it on the table for anyone to inspect.

THE NINE PILE

As a follow-up to the previous trick, switch to a prepared deck and rattle out this quick but effective piece of flim-flam. Write 'You will choose the nine pile' on a piece of paper, fold it and put it on your table. Now put three piles of cards on the table. Unbeknownst to the spectator, one pile contains just four nines, the second pile is of any nine cards, and the third pile consists of a five, a three and an ace (which add up to nine). Ask a spectator to choose any pile. You then open your prediction. Whichever pile is chosen your prediction will always be correct.

EXPERT TIP

Make sure that you never use the same cards for magic and for playing games. Playing games makes the cards limp, dirty and sticky. Cards used for magic should be crisp and clean, and easy to handle.

Predictive Power

Another feat of your special powers. Announce to your spectators, 'You will assist in an amazing demonstration of mindpower.'

Memorize a card (say the eight of Diamonds) and place it at the bottom of the deck. Spread the deck out, face down, noting where the eight of Diamonds goes. Choose a victim, and say, 'Point to the eight of Diamonds, or where you think it might be.'

He is unlikely to point to the right card. Pick up the card he does point to, without showing it to him. Let's suppose it is the six of Hearts. Now say, 'Point to the six of Hearts, or where you think it might be.'

Ask him to repeat this exercise, always without showing the card, always asking for the last card you have already picked up, until

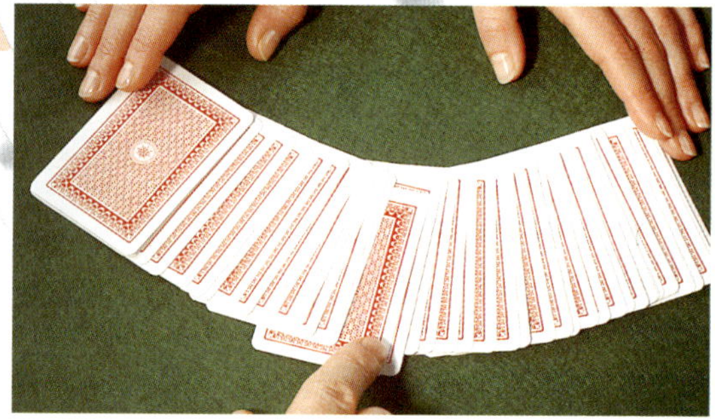

▲ *Ask the spectator to point to the eight of Diamonds.*

▼ *Mix up the four chosen cards.*

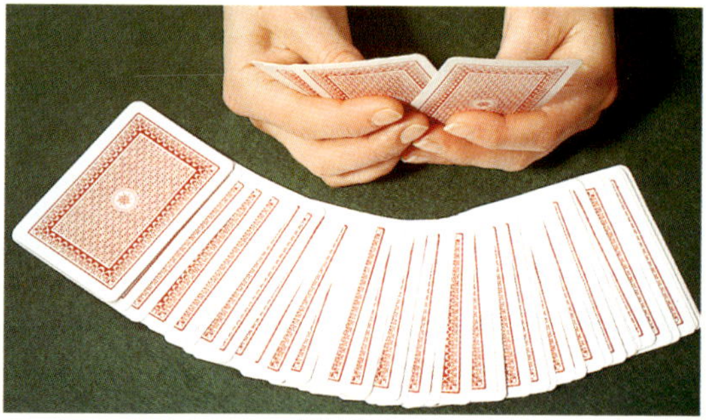

NOTE:
If the spectator, in a 1 in 52 chance, picks up the right card first time, congratulate him on his mental powers and move on to a different trick.

▶ *Lay out the four cards you called for.*

he has pointed to, and you have gathered up, three cards. Mix the three , still not showing them. Now say to the spectator, 'You have done very well, but I can go one better—I will pick up the correct card for the last one you pointed to.' You then pick up your eight of Diamonds.

Now you can lay out the cards one at a time to show how they correspond to the cards you asked for.

EXPERT TIPS ♥ ♣ ♦ ♠ ♥ ♣ ♦ ♠ ♥ ♣ ♦ ♠ ♥ ♣

- ***Never repeat a trick. When a trick works well you may be asked to 'do it again'. Don't. Do another trick instead.***
- ***All tricks should be practised in private before showing them to anyone. Never perform a trick if you have not practised it thoroughly.***

Count on It

Make the numbers work for you as you correctly predict the next card—before it is turned over.

Take a standard deck and let a spectator shuffle it, and another cut it. 'How many cards in this deck?' you ask. Back comes the answer, 'Fifty-two.' 'And what is half of fifty-two?' 'Twenty-six.'

You get a spectator to count off 26 cards face up. Memorize the seventh card in the sequence. Once the 26 are counted out, ask a spectator to turn them over in a single packet, face down. Then get the spectator to put the remaining half of the deck face down, and turn over the top card.

Now tell the spectator you want three piles of cards, each with a value of ten, made up by taking the value of the first card in the pile and adding the requisite number of cards (whatever their value) to reach ten. For example, if the first card turned over was a three, he would have to add seven cards. If it was a ten, he would leave it and start a fresh pile. In this exercise, aces count as one, court cards as ten.

Once you have the three piles, get the spectator to place the remaining cards face down on top of the pile of 26 cards that was counted out at the start, and to hold the whole packet in his hand.

Add the values of the three base cards in the three piles. Suppose they are five, seven, eight, totalling twenty. Deduct one, making it nineteen. Ask the spectator to count down the packet in his hand until he reaches the nineteenth card. Tell him the next card he comes to will be—name the card you memorized as seventh in the original sequence.

Flip it Over

The spectator's chosen card jumps out of the deck and lands face up on the table.

Take a full deck of cards, ask a spectator to examine it carefully, then ask him to pick a card. Mark the card (see Sleight of Hand Techniques, page 15) and ask the spectator to replace it in the deck.

Shuffle the cards, then spread them between your hands so that the spectator can see they are well mixed. Really you are looking at the backs of the cards to find your secret mark. Cut the cards at this point so the marked card is at the top.

NOTE:
You'll need to practise just the right height and angle from which to drop the deck to get the results shown in the photograph.

Slide the card some way towards you so that about half of it sticks out from the deck. Then drop the deck from your extended and lowered arm, on to the table. The top card will flip over—and it's the one he chose.

Mind Bender

Spookily, the spectator's chosen card rises from the deck.

Riffle through the deck and ask a spectator to take out a card, look at it, and return it to you. Without looking at its face, hold it up between the knuckles of your index and middle fingers, so everyone can see it. What they can't see is that you are also bending the corner with your (hidden) thumb.

Place the card anywhere in the deck and shuffle freely. Take one card from the top and one from the bottom and place them before and after the marked card so that they stick out about half-way from the base of the deck. Hold the deck firmly and push these two cards back in—the card between will pop up and reveal itself as the card selected by the spectator.

▲▼ *As you show the card, use your thumb to bend the corner.*

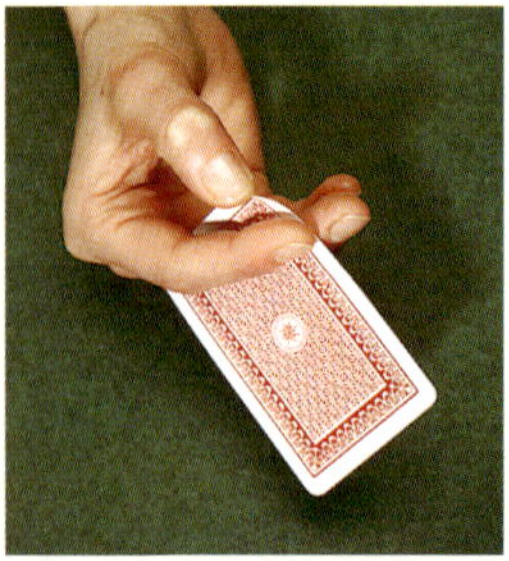

▲ *As you push the cards in, the prepared card will pop up.*

▲ *Reveal the card.*

Clip a Card

A two-second quickie, requiring no skill at all, but quite mystifying to the spectator—for a moment or two, anyway.

You show a set of five cards to a spectator and ask him to put a paper clip over one of them—he can't do it.

HOW:

You take five cards, preferably with a different colour in the middle (e.g. red, red, black, red, red).

Glue them together as shown, so that one card is fully face-on and the others show about a paper-clip's width.

Show the set to the spectator and ask him to agree they are perfectly normal cards. Ask him particularly to remember where the middle card is.

Then turn the set face down and ask him to place the clip over the middle card. Once he has done so, turn the deck face-forward again. He will find that the paper clip is not over the middle card but over the full-face one.

Red and Black

Can a spectator sort a deck into black and red, face down, without looking?

This trick requires some preparation. You take a standard deck of cards and arrange them face up in this way: 1 red, followed by 2 black, and a further red; then 24 red cards and 24 black cards.

Now take the prepared deck in your left hand and hold it up. You know the sequence of colours. Say to a chosen spectator: 'Could you sort this deck into reds and blacks, without looking?' Of course he will say no. But you say, 'Maybe you can. Let's see.' And at the same time you lay the top red card face up on the table, and place the next, black, card to its right. Put the next card, black again, overlapping the first black card. Then do the same with the fourth, red, card so that you have a black and a red pile already started.

▲ *You start red and black piles.*

Assure the spectator that, with your telepathic help, he will indeed be able to deal red and black piles without looking at the faces of the cards. First, however, you pick up one of the black cards on the table and place it in the top half of the deck; and a red card and place it in the lower half of the deck. A black and a red remain on the table.

'Those are guide cards,' you tell the spectator. 'Let your feel for colour take over, and deal cards on to the guide cards, face down. The columns don't have to have equal numbers of cards. Take your time, don't hurry.'

▲ *'How did you do it?'*

He deals the cards face down onto the markers according to what colour he thinks each card is. As he deals the 24th card you stop him and take the deck. 'Hold on,' you say. 'I want to make this harder by shuffling the remaining cards.' Of course, you know that you have one red and 24 black cards in your hand. Shuffle them. Looking through the cards in your hand (hiding them from the spectator) you take out the one red and place it face up on the right-hand (black) pile.

Pretend to search for a black card, then take one and place it face up on the left-hand (red) pile. Give the remaining cards back to the spectator and ask him to carry on. He deals out cards (face down) until the deck is finished.

'Now let's see,' you say. You scoop up all the right-hand cards except for the very first black guide card. Hold them in your left hand.

'Well, well,' you say (or something to the same effect) as you thumb off the top, face-down cards into your right hand, stopping when you reach the red marker. Turn these cards face up and spread them on the table: 'How interesting. All black,' Now remove the red marker and place it face up on the table. Turn up the remaining cards and spread them. 'All red. How did you do it?'

Now you can turn the left-hand pile face up and spread the cards beneath their respective markers to repeat the effect.

NOTE:
It helps a lot if you can let your spectators examine a standard deck at the start, then switch it for your set-up deck.

The Mystic Crystal Ball

You find a spectator's chosen card in the heart of a crystal ball.

For this trick you need a small crystal ball, or something that fulfills the same function. It must be reasonably transparent.

Have the crystal ball in your left-hand pocket. Give the deck of cards to a spectator to shuffle, then turn your back and have him put any card between your hands, face down.

Concealing your action, tear one of the index corners off the card. Holding the detached corner between the tips of the first and second fingers of your left hand, put that hand into the pocket containing the crystal ball.

Bring out the crystal ball with the corner of the card

▲ *Take a firm grasp of the corner.*

▼ *Tear off the corner.*

NOTE:
Most card tricks work best with new or pristine decks. This is a good trick for using with an old or incomplete deck.

◀ *The mystic crystal reveals all.*

face up underneath it. Gaze fixedly into the crystal ball. After great apparent effort, you tell first the colour, then the suit, then the value. Replace the crystal ball and the torn-off corner in your pocket, and display the card, covering the torn-off corner with your finger. Drop the card into your right-hand pocket as soon as possible.

▶ *Having named the card, produce it with a flourish, being sure to cover up the torn corner!*

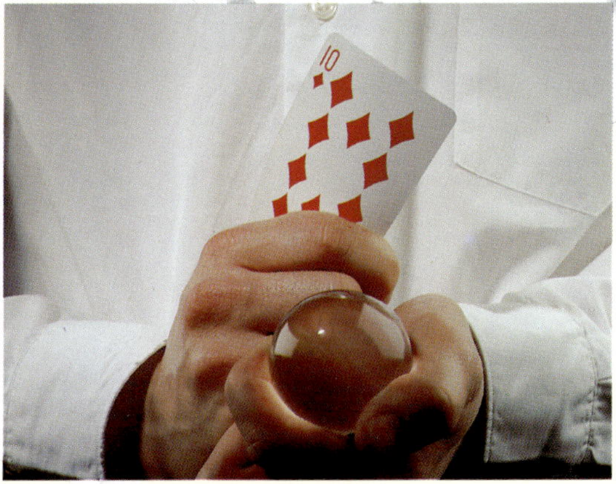

Glass Magic

With a few simple props, you can produce a classic illusionist's trick.

For this trick you need two decks, a large long-stemmed glass, a linen napkin, and a little bit of manual dexterity. You are going to make all four aces appear in sequence from the deck.

'I shall use my special locator cards to draw out the aces,' you say. Reaching into the glass, you extract a red card, say the ten of Diamonds, and place it at the front of the deck, where all can see it through the glass. Now take the glass by the stem and drape the napkin momentarily over it. When you take the napkin off, the ace of Diamonds has replaced the ten. Take the ace and put it at the back of the deck and repeat the pass with the napkin. Now the spectators see the ace of Hearts. Extract another locator card, black this time, say the four of Spades. Make a rapid pass with the napkin, and reveal the ace of Spades. A further pass reveals the ace of Clubs. Extract the deck and return it to your card-case.

HOW:

Prepare your deck as follows: glue the two red aces back-to-back, and do the same with the two black aces. Take out the ten of Diamonds and the four of Spades. From an identical deck take the ten of Diamonds and four of Spades.

◀ *Show the ten of Diamonds.*

▶ *Rotate the glass under cover of the napkin.*

Glue a ten of Diamonds and a four of Spades together, back-to-back.

Set up your deck like this: the black four face up on top of the face-down deck, with the double-sided black ace on top of it. Now place the double-sided red ten/black four card with the red ten side face up. Next come the double-sided red aces. Finally, place the red ten face down. Place the deck in the glass, with the bottom card showing to the spectator. The prepared cards are at the bottom, facing you.

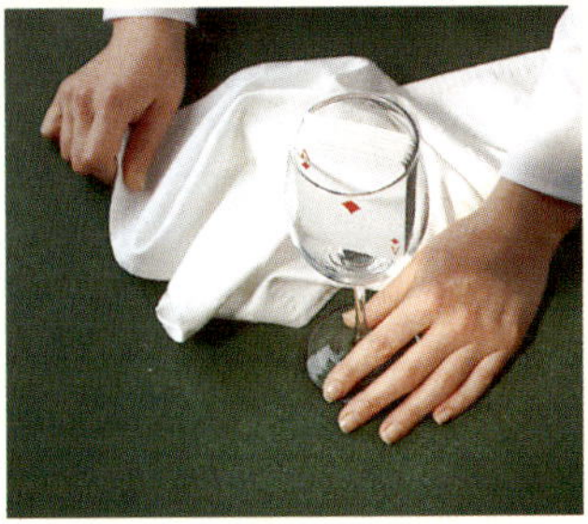

▲ *Show the first ace. Rotate the glass under cover of the napkin as in the previous step.*
▼ *Show the next ace.*

Take out the bottom card (red ten), show it and place at the top. The ace of Diamonds is now facing you. As you drape the napkin over the glass, turn it in your hand, so that the ace is presented to the spectators when you whisk away the napkin.

Take the ace, being careful to show only one face, and replace it at the bottom of the deck, so that the ace of Hearts side is facing you. Repeating the napkin pass, show it to the spectators. Now say, 'Let's see if I can find a locator for the black aces.' Lift the black/red card, with the four of Spades showing, from the side of the deck facing you. Place it at the front so that the ace of Spades is now facing you.

NOTE:
If anyone wants to see the deck, you will need to have a standard deck to switch.

Repeat the pass and the turn, and present the ace of Spades. Take it out, place it on the top, and the final black ace is waiting for you to repeat the manoeuvre.

Window Mystery

This dramatic trick is ideal for an evening performance in a private home—but it will work best on the ground floor.

Stand in front of a window with curtains pulled. Invite a spectator to choose a card from the deck, examine and memorize it, then replace it. Shuffle the deck, looking pensive and uncertain. Then suddenly toss the deck against the curtains. As the spectator reassembles the deck, he finds his card is missing. 'Draw the curtains back, and you'll find it,' you say.

He draws the curtains back, and the card is found sticking to the outside of the window-pane.

HOW:

The chosen card is in fact forced (see Sleight of Hand Techniques, page 14). In advance, you have stuck a duplicate of the card on the outside of the pane, using transparent double-sided tape.

As you receive the deck back from the spectator, note where he places the chosen card, shuffle it to the top, and palm it off before you toss the rest of the deck at the curtains.

Get Thee Behind Me

A reverse-card trick in which the spectator does all the hard work.

Here you get a spectator to work the trick himself—with his hands behind his back. Use a standard deck, and present it to a spectator for checking and shuffling. Ask him to cut it into two packets, one of which he hands to you, and the other he keeps.

Ask him to examine his packet, select a card, memorize it, and place it as top card in the packet, face down. As he does this, you turn away, reversing two cards in your own packet—the bottom one and the one second from the top. You don't need to note what they are. Turning back, place your packet in the spectator's hand above his own. Your reversed bottom card is now immediately above his chosen card. Square the deck in his hand, tell him to hold it tightly and place it behind his back:

'Now you're going to try to locate the card you chose—without looking.'

Once the deck is behind his back, tell him to take off the top card, then change your mind—use some excuse. 'Maybe you think it's been rigged, why don't you put that card to the bottom? Now take the next card underneath, turn it over, and put it into the middle of the deck.'

Now ask him to bring the deck forward. Of course, by reversing the second card, he has put it the same way round as all the others—except your bottom card. Naturally he thinks that is the card he inserted, and he is amazed to find it just above the card he chose at the beginning.

The Three-card Trick

A version of the street sharper's legendary method of parting passers-by from their cash. But this is purely for fun!

To work this, you need an accomplice (prearranged and unknown to the other spectators). You hold three cards, two plain cards and a court card, face down, one plain one between the second finger and thumb of your left hand The other two, one of which should be the court card, should be held between the first finger and thumb and second finger and thumb of your right hand. The cards should not be new.

▲ *All you have to do is to find the lady …*

Bring your hands quickly together, then apart, and drop the three cards in very rapid succession, face down. Ask the bystanders to identify the court card. At this stage they have a one-in-three chance of being right. But after a few tries, while you allow your attention to be diverted, your accomplice winks to the others and sneakily bends up a corner of the court card.

Gathering up the cards again, you apparently don't notice. In fact, with the bent corner hidden between the third and fourth fingers of your right hand, you straighten the bend and instead bend the corner of one of the others. Now, as you drop the cards, everyone will pick on the bent card, and be amazed to see it is the wrong one.

▶ *Deal the three cards face down.*

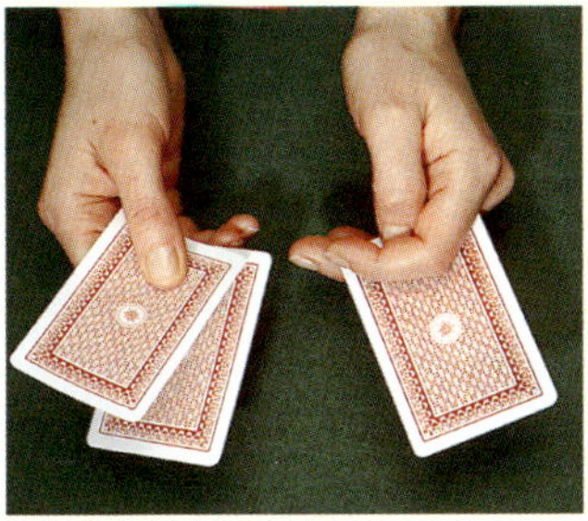

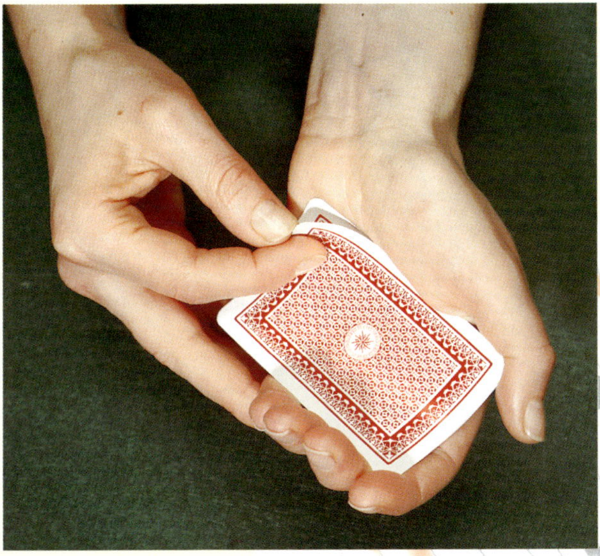

▲ *A 'spectator' (actually your accomplice) bends a corner of the court card.*

◀ *As you gather up the cards, straighten the bent card and bend a corner of one of the other cards.*

EXPERT TIP ♥ ♣ ♦ ♠ ♥ ♣ ♦ ♠ ♥ ♣ ♦ ♠ ♥ ♣

Use a pair of nail clippers to trim a small piece from the diagonally opposite corners of one card. This makes an excellent locator card. Riffle down a corner of the deck and you feel and hear the locator card so you can find it, and the (chosen) card next to it, with ease.

Inseparable Aces

However far apart in the deck they are, the four aces will always come together at your command.

Use a standard deck, and invite your spectators to inspect and shuffle it. Then remove the four aces, hand them to a spectator, and ask him to replace them on top of the deck. Now secretly transfer the three bottom cards of the deck—it does not matter what they are—on top of the aces. You can do this by the pass (see page 12) or by using cards palmed (see page 11) while everyone is examining the aces.

You announce that you will place each of the aces in completely different parts of the deck. Lift off the four top cards, being careful to display only the true ace and concealing the three others behind it.

Lay them face down on the table, then insert each very obviously into different parts of the deck. Make sure that you insert the real ace as third or fourth from the

▶ *Transfer three bottom cards to the top of the deck.*

▶ *Display the true ace with three bottom cards hidden behind.*

top, and that the nondescript cards are placed out of the way. At this point you have all four aces at the top, and can simply hand the deck to a spectator to find them.

To make the effect more dramatic, ask a spectator to cut the deck for you. Take the two packets in your left hand, the tip of your little finger separating them (the aces are now at the top of the lower packet). You can now say, 'I will order the four aces to come together. Would you prefer them to be at the top of the deck, or in the centre? I know in advance which you will choose, and the aces are already in position.'

If they choose the centre, simply withdraw the little fingertip. If they choose the top, make the pass to bring them there.

EXPERT TIP ♥ ♣ ♦ ♠ ♥ ♣ ♦ ♠ ♥ ♣ ♦ ♠ ♥ ♣

Don't bore your audience by doing too many tricks at any one time. Always leave your audience wanting more.

Infallible Prediction

The spectator picks up the card you predict—every time. The cheat is so outrageous that your audience will never guess!

For this you need two decks: one standard deck, which you keep in your pocket, and one set-up deck. On this deck you write: 'This is the card you will choose' down the right-hand side of every card except two, which you place on the top and bottom of the deck.

Shuffle this deck without moving the top and bottom cards, and show the bottom card to the spectators. Pretend to write something down the right-hand side of one of the middle cards, then shuffle again, bringing the top card to the bottom and showing this one, too, to the spectators. Now

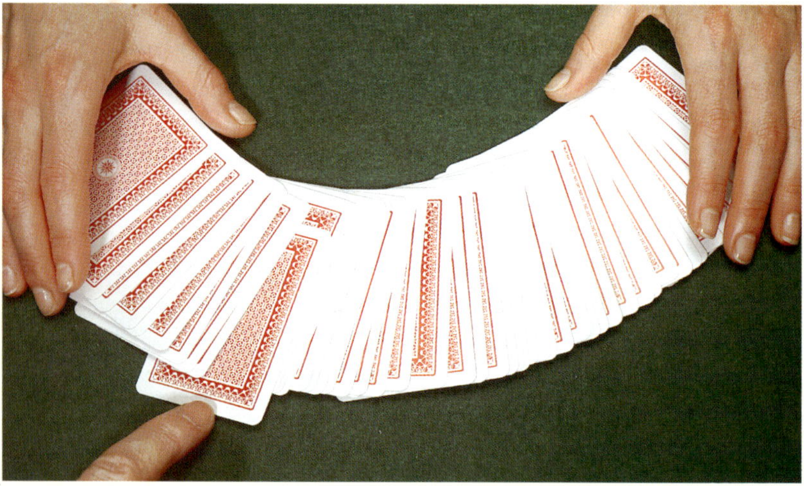

▲ *Pick any card—except the top and bottom card.*

spread the deck out face down on the table and invite a spectator to draw one out, without looking at it.

▲ *The effect: the spectator has unnervingly selected the predicted card !*

Gather up the others, and open them in such a way that the right-hand sides are hidden, and show them to the spectators, explaining that you are looking for the one you wrote the message on—but it clearly isn't there. Invite the spectator who chose the card on the table to turn it over. Naturally it bears your message.

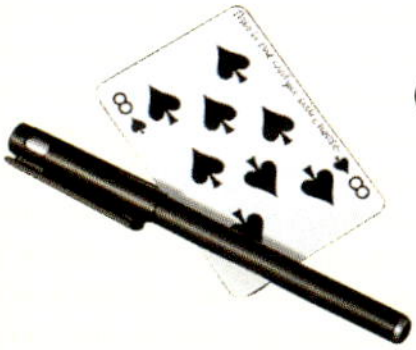

Casually drop the deck into your pocket and proceed quickly to do another trick with the standard deck.

NOTE:
There is a minimal chance of the spectator picking the unmarked end cards. If you keep your hands close to them, the spectator will tend to avoid them and select from an inner location. Use this tip for other tricks, too.

EXPERT TIP ♥ ♣
Carry a deck of cards with you at all times so you are always ready to do a trick should someone ask.

Double Speller

One of the numerous tricks based on the number of letters in a card's name (e.g. two of Spades = 11; seven of Diamonds = 15).

Shuffle the deck and give it to a spectator, asking him to deal it out into four piles, face down. Ask him then to take the top or bottom card of any pile, memorize it, and replace it in its original position.

Ask a second spectator to do the same. Now you take the four piles and reassemble them into a complete deck.

Ask one spectator to name the card he memorized. You proceed to spell it out, dealing a card face up for every letter. As you spell out the final 's', you turn up the very card he named.

HOW:

Prepare the deck by placing the three of Hearts, seven of Hearts, queen of Hearts and queen of Spades in any order, on the top; and the four, five, jack and king of Diamonds on the bottom.

When you shuffle (riffle shuffle) do not move the positions of these cards. When the spectator deals out his four piles, one card from the Hearts group

▲ *The spectator deals out four piles face down.*

(13 letters) will be at the bottom of each pile; and one of the other group (14 letters) at the top.

Observe which pile is which, and whether your victims took cards from the top or bottom. Suppose your first victim picked a bottom card, put that pile on top as you assemble the deck; then count down to the correct card (a Heart). If the other victim has picked a top card, place one of the two untouched piles on top of it, and add the second untouched pile underneath. This enables you to count down fourteen cards, arriving at the correct one (a Diamond).

Number Force

Another countdown corker to stun your audience.

Spread the deck face up to show that all the cards are different. Secretly memorize the ninth card from the top.

Turn the deck face down and ask for any number between ten and nineteen. Deal that number of cards, one at a time, onto the table. Pick up the dealt pile. Add the digits of the chosen number and now deal that number of cards from the pile onto the table. The next card will be the one you memorized.

Coin Calculation

To complete this calculating trio of number tricks, demonstrate a strange connection between a coin and a card.

Place a standard deck on the table. Invite a spectator to take out a coin and write down its date, then its date in reverse. Suppose the date is 1997, which reverses to 7991. Ask him then to subtract the smaller figure from the larger. This gives 5994. Now ask him to remove four cards from the deck, of a different suit in each case, with the same pip value as the four numbers of the answer. If a zero is included, use a king. During all this process, make sure you keep your back to him.

Tell the spectator to place the four cards face down and move them around until he

▲ *Get the spectator to move the cards around.*

▶ *Practise your mental arithmetic—this trick always works!*

▶ *Sneak a look at the discards.*

no longer remembers which is which; then to take one and put it in his pocket, without looking at it.

Now you turn round. Holding the deck in your left hand, pick up his three remaining cards, and as you add them to the deck, glance secretly at their face value. First note which suit is missing, then add up their values and subtract the total from the nearest multiple of nine. Suppose the three cards are the five of Clubs, nine of Diamonds and nine of Spades, adding up to twenty-three. The nearest multiple of nine is twenty-seven. The missing suit is Hearts. Subtracting twenty-three from twenty-seven, you say, 'The card in your pocket is the four of Hearts.'

The effect is all the more satisfactory since, until he brings it out, the spectator himself does not know.

If you want to promote social embarrassment among the more mature spectators, a variant of this trick is Birthdays, when you ask the spectator to write down his or her birth year.

EXPERT TIP ♥ ♣ ♦ ♠ ♥ ♣ ♦ ♠ ♥ ♣ ♦ ♠ ♥ ♣

Don't tell anyone how the tricks are done. Keep the methods secret. If a trick goes wrong, don't panic. Just stop doing that trick and move quickly on to another one.

The Turnabout Card

A particular card magically turns itself upside-down in the deck—simplicity itself.

Present a deck to the spectator and ask him to select a card, and memorize it, then replace it somewhere in the middle of the deck (which is still in your hand). When he has done so, spread the cards. Only one card is face up, and that is the one he selected.

HOW:

Prepare your deck with all cards face down except for the bottom one, which is face up. While the spectator is examining his card, secretly turn over the deck. Now all the cards are face up, except for the top one, which is face down. Seeing this, the spectator naturally supposes that all the cards are face down, and replaces his in the same fashion. All you need to do is take the deck behind your back and secretly turn over the top card (the card you reversed earlier). Turn the deck over in your hands. Say you are trying to locate the chosen card and reverse it. Bring the deck forward and spread out the cards. Just one card is face up—the spectator's chosen card!

▲ *Card goes into reversed stack.*

▲ *Fan the deck to show the card!*

Odds and Evens

Fool your audience with this shamefully easy trick.

From the standard deck, place on the table two piles of cards, not too neatly, each with the same even number of cards (any cards will do). Six and eight are the best numbers to use. Tell your spectators that one pile contains an even number of cards, the other an odd number (this is not true). Say, 'I won't tell you which pile is which, but I can confidently predict that each time you try to say which pile is which, you will be wrong. Every single time.'

▲ *Keep a card palmed to stack the odds in your favour.*

▼ *Right again!*

The spectators will rise to your challenge. Meanwhile, your right hand has palmed a single card from the top of the deck, which you had placed face down on the table. When the spectators have decided which pile is the even one, you pick up that pile with the right hand, to count it, and drop the palmed card on top, instantly making it odd. If the spectators choose to identify the odd pile, you simply pick it up with your left hand, spreading the cards with your splayed-out right fingers, to show it is even.

Then bring the two piles together, adding the extra card if it is still palmed, and replace the cards on the table.

Magic in my Pocket

After apparently getting it wrong, you produce the spectator's chosen card from your pocket.

Hand a standard deck of cards to a spectator, and ask him to shuffle it thoroughly. Ask him to think of a number, and count down through the cards, holding the deck face down, until he reaches the number, then to inspect and memorize the card at that place. Then he should replace it in the deck. While he does this, keep your back towards him. When he is ready, turn round, and take the deck.

▲ *The spectator chooses a card.*

Ask the victim to concentrate mentally on his card and its location. Take the deck in your left hand and move it behind your back, indicating great mental effort on your own part as you do so.

Bring forward the bottom card in your right hand, with its face towards yourself. Hesitate for effect, then apparently thrust this card into your right-hand trouser pocket.

▲ *'Is this your card?'*

▲ *Produce the palmed queen from your pocket.*

▲ *'I have the right card in my pocket.'*

In reality you palm it, and place it on top of the deck as you transfer the deck from your left hand to your right.

'If I am right,' you say, 'I now have your card in my pocket. Now, tell me the number you first thought of, but not what the card was.'

Suppose he says it was six. Deal five cards rapidly, face down, then toss the sixth towards him, face down, saying, 'Is this your card?'

While he, and everyone else, is looking at this card, your left thumb pushes the next card over the side of the deck and your right hand comes back, palms it, and slides it into your trouser pocket.

'Of course it's not,' you continue. 'How can it be, when I have the right card in my pocket?'

Bring out the card, face towards you, and ask him to name it, then turn it to show it really is the card he selected.

EXPERT TIP

Palming is such an important technique for the card magician that it's well worth extra practice in front of a mirror until your palming is as undetectable as possible.

Four King Lift

However far the four kings are separated in the shuffle, they always meet in the royal suite at the top of the deck.

This curiously named trick is a popular one. In some versions the story-line is different, but the underlying principle is always the same. Explain to your audience that the deck of cards is like a multi-storey hotel, with a lift in it. Wherever you place the four kings in the building, they will always take the lift together to reach their proper position in the royal suite on the top floor.

▲ *Separate the four kings.*

Separate the four kings from the rest of the deck and shuffle the deck vigorously. Now, bring the kings together at the top of the deck, fan them out enough to

◀ *Four kings apparently at the top of the deck—but hide four other cards exactly behind the top king.*

show they are indeed the kings, and say, 'Here they are, in the royal suite. Now I'll move them down.'

Close the deck. Move one king to the basement (bottom of the deck); another to the lobby (near the bottom); another to the dining room (middle) and the fourth to the fitness club (in the upper half but not on top). Now say, 'You've seen the kings all placed in different parts of the hotel. But will they stay there? Not them. Up they go, in the lift.' Tap the edge of the closed deck against the table, and pass it to the nearest spectator to examine. All four kings are at the top.

▲ *Moving the dummy cards from the top.*

HOW:

Start with the four kings fanned out in your left hand at the top of the deck. Shuffle the rest of the deck. But palm four additional cards into your left hand and conceal them exactly behind the top king. When you close the deck, hold it face down in your right hand, sloping away from you slightly, and move the cards with your left. Instead of moving the kings, you move the unseen four cards that have come to the top as you closed the fan. To bring this trick off to maximum effect, you'll need to practise the precise positioning of the unseen cards.

EXPERT TIP ♥ ♣ ♦ ♠ ♥ ♣ ♦ ♠ ♥ ♣ ♦ ♠ ♥ ♣

Dust cards with zinc stearate to make them slippery and easier to handle. Magicians call it 'fanning powder' and it can be bought under this name from magic shops.

Toppers

Let the spectators freely shuffle the deck, and deal it into four piles. You will name the top card in each pile.

Take the deck yourself. Shuffle the deck and palm off the bottom card in your right hand. Now offer the deck to a spectator and ask him to give it a really thorough shuffle, and then to pass it to another spectator for the same treatment again. This gives you the chance to look at (secretly) the palmed card and memorize it.

Now take back the deck into your right hand and replace the palmed card on top, saying, 'As you have shuffled the whole deck, I have no means of knowing which card is which—except for my mental powers. Would someone be kind enough to cut the deck into four parts and set them out on the table in front of me, and I will name the top card of each pile.'

▲ *After you have shuffled the deck, palm off the bottom card in your right hand.*

When the piles are set out, note where the pile with the top card of the deck is. Suppose this card is the queen of Clubs. Now take the top card, face down, from another pile, looking as if you are concentrating hard, and say, keeping the card hidden from the spectators, 'This is the queen of Clubs.'

▲ *Sneak a look at the pickup cards.*

▲ *You have named all four cards.*

Take a rapid glance at what the card really is, for example, the nine of Spades, and select the top card of another pile, saying 'This is . . . the nine of Spades.' Again, you hide it from the spectators while glancing at it yourself and seeing it is, for example, the four of Hearts.

You pick up from the top of the third pile and say, 'This is the four of Hearts.' Actually, you see it is the ace of Diamonds. It only remains now to pick up the card you have known all along to be the queen of Clubs, and say, possibly mopping your brow because of the mental effort, 'This is the ace of Diamonds.'

Now flourish all four cards to your spectators so that they see your prediction is correct, without knowing which card came from which pile.

Elimination

The irresistible force of your mind will make a spectator turn up two cards memorized earlier.

Deal thirty cards from a standard deck onto the table, in six packets of five. Set aside the rest of the deck, face down, and invite a spectator to take any two cards from it. He must memorize these two cards, then place them face down on top of two of the six piles.

▲ *The spectator selects two cards from the deck and adds them to two of the six packets.*

Now you take up all six packets and deal them out into two piles. Invite the spectator to choose one of these piles and to deal it out, card by card, into two further piles of eight cards each.

Ignoring one of the piles, ask him to deal out the other into two further piles of four cards each, and repeat until only two packets, each with two cards, remain. The spectator now finds he has chosen the two cards he was asked to memorize.

HOW:

Note which packets have the spectator's cards on top. Take the one with the first card, and place two untouched packets on top. Place the two remaining packets on top of the one with the second chosen card.

▲ *Deal the cards into two piles of eight cards.*

▲ *The final two piles of two cards; turning up the correct cards.*

Now you have two packets of sixteen. Bring them together; it does not matter which is on top. Deal the cards into two equal piles, one card to each pile alternately. Both of the chosen cards will be in the pile to which the first card of the sixteen is dealt. Steer the spectator to deal from this pile.

Ask the spectator to deal out the eight cards into two equal packets of four. Again the chosen cards will be in the pile to which the first card is dealt. Then ask him to deal out the four into two packets of two. The chosen cards will be in the pile to which the first card is dealt. This trick needs pace and patter to be carried out most effectively. Keep your piles nice and tidy and don't forget which pile held the chosen cards at the start.

EXPERT TIP ♥ ♣ ♦ ♠ ♥ ♣ ♦ ♠ ♥ ♣ ♦ ♠ ♥ ♣

If you find your cards have become dirty, the easiest way to clean them is by using a piece of bread. Roll the bread into a small ball and rub it over the surface of the card. All but the deepest of stains will be removed.

Princess

Without any possibility of knowing which card a spectator has chosen, you produce it triumphantly from your pocket.

Use a standard deck and invite a spectator to inspect and shuffle it. Take the deck back, spread it face up and invite four spectators each to select one card, the first being any Club, the second any Heart, the third any Spade and the last any Diamond. Now palm the three top cards from the deck in your right hand and retain the deck in the same hand.

Hold out your left hand and ask the spectators to lay their four cards on your palm, face-down, in the opposite order to their selection. Lay the deck on the table, and transfer the four cards to your right hand, adding the three palmed cards.

Square up all seven and hold them in your hand, the bottom card facing the audience, with your thumb at the bottom and fingers crooked over the top. With your left hand, slowly separate the four chosen cards, keeping the palmed cards completely hidden behind the Club card.

Ask a spectator mentally to select any of the four, then close the fan and turn the packet to face yourself.

▶ *Fan out the chosen cards—but keep the palmed card hidden behind the Club card.*

▲ *Pretend to select 'one' card from the four—in fact it is all four cards together.*

▲ *Slip the 'single' card into your pocket. You know the sequence, so it is simple to produce the right card later.*

Still with the packet facing you, fan out four cards, but this time it is the three palmed cards that you open, with the four chosen cards grouped as one. With an expression of great mental exertion, draw out one of the single cards, hesitate, and replace it in a different location in the fan. Repeat with another single card, and finally take the four-as-one card and put 'it' in your outside right-hand pocket.

Count the three remaining cards face down on to the deck and cut them into the middle. Say, 'I believe I have your selected card in my pocket. Will you be so kind as to name it.'

When he names it, you have only to reach into your pocket, where the four cards are in Clubs/Hearts/Spades/Diamonds sequence, and, with a suitable flourish, draw out the appropriate one.

Super Count-down

This trick requires a prearranged deck, and like other similar tricks, it benefits from your being able to present a standard deck for inspection, then switching to the set-up one.

Secretly arrange the deck in the sequence red-black-red-black-red, etc. Values do not matter. Hand the deck to a spectator, asking, 'Which do you prefer, odds or evens?'

If he says 'Odds', ask him to think of any odd number between one and 21. Then, while your back is turned, he is to cut the deck several times, then count off a pile of cards up to the number he has decided on, and memorize the next card. He should put this card on top of the cards he has dealt, then put

▲ *The spectator memorizes a card.*

▲ *The final cut.*

the rest of the deck on top of that—all face down. Finally, he should cut the deck again, only this time ask him to cut the cards 'roughly in half.'

Now you turn round, pick up the deck and fan it out, facing you, and observe where two cards of the same color come together. Cut here, sending one to the top of the deck and the other to the bottom.

▲ *Count aloud through the deck.*

Run through the cards again, counting as you do so, until you again reach two of the same color together. The first of these will be the card memorized by the spectator. The number of cards you have counted is the number he first thought of.

If he says 'Evens', ask him to think of any even number between two and twenty. While your back is turned, he should count that number of cards off the deck—but instead of memorizing the next card in the deck, he should turn over, memorize, and replace the top card of the pile he has just dealt.

NOTE:
It is important that the number chosen at the beginning of the trick must be less than half the deck and the final cutting must be no more than half—so choose your wording carefully.

The cards are then cut (approximately in half) and you continue as before. This time, however, the number of cards counted must include the chosen card to arrive at the number selected by the spectator.

Useful Books

There are lots of excellent books on card magic. Try your local library or bookshop to see what is available. The following are especially recommended:

Encyclopedia of Card Tricks edited by Jean Hugard, Faber & Faber, London, 1974. *In its time this was the most comprehensive work on the subject and, although new techniques have been developed, this book should still be studied by anyone who wishes to learn about card magic.*

World's Best Card Tricks by Bob Longe, Sterling Publishing Co Inc., New York, 1992. *A useful collection from a prolific author.*

Card Tricks by Peter Eldin, Funfax, Woodbridge, 1994. *Written especially for children.*

Master Magician by Sandy Ransford, Apple Press, London, 1994.

Performing Card and Magic Tricks by Jon Tremaine, Simon & Schuster, Hemel Hempstead, 1994.

Magic Dealers

Specialist magic dealers include:

International Magic Studio, 89 Clerkenwell Road, London, EC1R 5BX, UK.

American Magic Co., AMC House, 44 Rutherford Road, Windle, Merseyside, WA10 6JH, UK.

Hey Presto Magic Shop, Sydney, Australia. Tel no: (2) 9232 7660.

Abracadabra Magic, Melbourne, Australia. Tel no: (3) 9804 0720.

Magic Clubs

The Magic Circle, 12 Stephenson Way, London, NW1 2HD. *Founded in 1905, this is the organization for serious practitioners of conjuring. It sponsors the biennial Young Magician of the Year competition. Associate membership is possible. Information on the Magic Circle's activities and publications is available from the Secretary.*

International Brotherhood of Magicians, P.O. Box 192090, St Louis, MO 63119-9998, USA. *The headquarters are in the USA but members from all countries are welcome.*